IT'S TIME TO EAT BAKED CHICKEN

It's Time to Eat BAKED CHICKEN

Walter the Educator

SKB
Silent King Books
A WhichHead Entertainment Imprint

Copyright © 2024 by Walter the Educator

All rights reserved. No part of this book may be reproduced in any manner whatsoever without written per- mission except in the case of brief quotations embodied in critical articles and reviews.

First Printing, 2024

Disclaimer

This book is a literary work; the story is not about specific persons, locations, situations, and/or circumstances unless mentioned in a historical context. Any resemblance to real persons, locations, situations, and/or circumstances is coincidental. This book is for entertainment and informational purposes only. The author and publisher offer this information without warranties expressed or implied. No matter the grounds, neither the author nor the publisher will be accountable for any losses, injuries, or other damages caused by the reader's use of this book. The use of this book acknowledges an understanding and acceptance of this disclaimer.

It's Time to Eat BAKED CHICKEN is a collectible early learning book by Walter the Educator suitable for all ages belonging to Walter the Educator's Time to Eat Book Series. Collect more books at WaltertheEducator.com

USE THE EXTRA SPACE TO TAKE NOTES AND DOCUMENT YOUR MEMORIES

BAKED CHICKEN

It's baked chicken time, hooray, hooray!

It's Time to Eat
Baked Chicken

Golden and yummy, fresh each day!

In the oven, warm and sweet,

Baked chicken is our favorite treat!

Tender bites, so soft and light,

With every taste, it feels just right.

It's juicy, tasty, full of fun

Baked chicken is number one!

Crunch, crunch, chew! It's fun to eat,

With veggies or rice, it's hard to beat!

Healthy, hearty, warm, and bright,

Baked chicken makes each bite just right!

With herbs and spices sprinkled around,

It fills the air, what a tasty sound!

From oven to plate, we watch it cook,

Just one whiff and we can't help but look!

It's Time to Eat
Baked Chicken

It's crispy outside, soft inside,

Baked chicken fills us up with pride!

Good for growing, good for play,

It's the best meal in every way!

Served with carrots, corn, or peas,

It's the dinner that's sure to please!

Cut it in pieces, big or small,

Baked chicken is loved by all!

Add some sauce, or have it plain,

It's warm and cozy, like sunshine rain.

For lunch, for dinner, every bite,

Baked chicken's perfect, warm, and light!

With every slice, we feel so strong,

Baked chicken helps us all day long!

From kitchen to plate, it's cooked with love,

It's Time to Eat
Baked Chicken

A tasty gift from the oven above!

So let's all cheer, let's all say,

"Baked chicken time is here today!"

Golden, juicy, baked to please,

It's the perfect meal for you and me!

Grab a fork, let's dig right in,

With baked chicken, we all win!

Healthy, yummy, soft, and fine,

It's Time to Eat

Baked Chicken

The perfect meal, it's baked chicken time!

ABOUT THE CREATOR

Walter the Educator is one of the pseudonyms for Walter Anderson. Formally educated in Chemistry, Business, and Education, he is an educator, an author, a diverse entrepreneur, and he is the son of a disabled war veteran.
"Walter the Educator" shares his time between educating and creating. He holds interests and owns several creative projects that entertain, enlighten, enhance, and educate, hoping to inspire and motivate you. Follow, find new works, and stay up to date with Walter the Educator™

at WaltertheEducator.com

Milton Keynes UK
Ingram Content Group UK Ltd.
UKHW020821141124
451205UK00012B/660